D1393204

ISLAY'S COASTLINE

A photographic tour of the coast of Islay

Becky Williamson

Published by

Green Bug Productions

Woodside Cottage
Gruinart, Isle of Islay
PA44 7PP
www.green-bug-productions.co.uk
info@green-bug-productions.co.uk

First published in 2011
Reprinted 2012

ISBN 978-1-907039-08-9

Printed in the United Kingdom

(Front page: Thrift and coast north-east of Sanaigmore.)

INTRODUCTION

I moved to the Isle of Islay in 2004 and, as is my want, began a perusal of the two explorer maps of the island, looking for places to walk. I have always been drawn towards the coast, so naturally I chose walks by the sea, rarely repeating the same walk twice as I wanted to familiarise myself with as much as possible of Islay's coastline.

In 2006 I read of a 'coastal challenge', promoted by Kate Humble, in which people were choosing an area of coastline to cover by human power to raise money for the Marine Conservation Society (MCS). In this way the MCS hoped to cover the UK's entire coastline. After a quick check of my now well-used and sellotaped-together maps, I realised that I had already walked about half of Islay's coastline. What a great incentive to walk the rest!

Time was not an issue for me. I have never seen the point in rushing a walk. I like to amble (telling myself I'm quite capable of going faster if I really want to!), taking photographs and looking all around me at the surrounding nature and scenery. Hence it took me about four years to complete the walk - so maybe not quite as fast as those who had gone before (I think they took a week!) but probably with more photos!

I finished on my 40th birthday on 6th May 2008. The grand finale was a walk of only about 50 feet, but it was nigh on the scariest and most difficult part of the walk for me as it involved traversing the swing bridge across the River Laggan at the north end of the Big Strand.

Islay has about 120 miles of coastline, but I walked a lot further than that as I often had to return to the car the way I had come, thus doubling the mileage for that particular stretch. Also, curiosity sometimes got the better of me ('I just HAVE to see what's over the top of that hill,' or 'I'll just take a wee peep round that corner.') Mostly I walked alone, but was glad of company on the odd occasion.

As mentioned earlier, one of the purposes of the walk was to raise money for the MCS, a charity which promotes the need for marine wildlife protection, sustainable fisheries and clean seas and beaches. Altogether

I raised about £500 for the work of the MCS. For more information about the MCS, visit http://www.mcsuk.org/.

For ease, the photos take a clockwise route, starting and finishing at Port Ellen. This is not how I did the walk; sometimes I walked clockwise, sometimes anti-clockwise. Also, although all the photos are my own, they are not necessarily taken on my first walk of the area they depict. I returned to some places many times, others I have visited only once so I have included photos of all seasons and weathers in order to provide a more complete picture of this beautiful part of the world.

I have included maps for like-minded map addicts, but apologise for the roughness of the maps and for their size. The maps are hand-drawn and I found it difficult to be 100 % accurate at times about the precise location of a photo. Also, the quality would be compromised if the maps were reproduced in a larger size. I hope you will excuse this and simply enjoy the photos, referring to the Ordnance Survey Explorer Maps for Islay North (No. 353) and Islay South (No. 352) for more detailed information.

A word of warning to would-be walkers - there are hardly any footpaths around Islay's coast. It was often VERY hard work trudging through bracken, heather and bog and crossing many a barbed wire fence. On one occasion I spent the night in a bothy (An Cladach) in order to walk to McArthur's Head and on another occasion in a tent (at Bolsa) to break up the walk a little. Access is not a problem in Scotland as there are no trespassing laws, but in some cases it is advisable, out of courtesy, to contact landowners or gamekeepers before beginning your walk. My walk was also hampered by my ever-present camera and binoculars which were permanently hung round my neck; I simply cannot conceive of going a walk without them.

I don't want to put anyone off though; hard work it may have been, but also incredibly rewarding as I hope the following pages show. If you are inspired to try something similar yourself and want more information, please get in touch (enquiries@solus-is-sith.co.uk).

See Islay's beauty for yourself - get out there and walk!

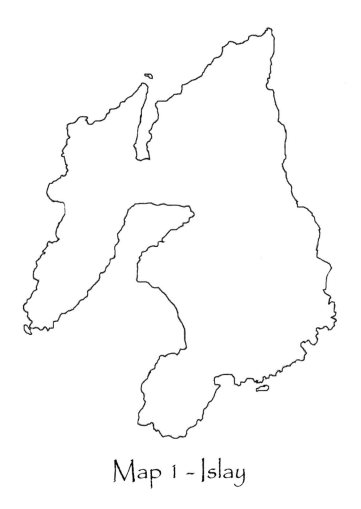

Map 1 - Islay

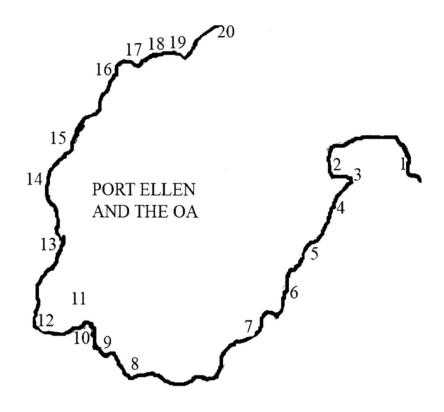

Map 2 - Port Ellen and The Oa

Port Ellen -
Loch Leòdamais. (1)

Kilnaughton Bay, looking towards Port Ellen.
It is rare to see the beaches on Islay covered with snow. (2)

Carraig Fhada
lighthouse, looking
towards
Eilean na Caorach
and Texa with the
Kintyre peninsula
on the mainland
in the distance. (3)

The Singing Sands and
Carraig Fhada lighthouse. (4)

Sea monster, Tràigh Bhàn
(Singing Sands). (4)

Port an Eas. (5)

Port an Eas. (5)

Looking back to Port an Eas from
Rubh ' a' Chlàdain. (6)

Sheep
near Stremnishmore. (7)

Dùn Athad and the American
Monument from Beinn Mhòr. (8)

Closer view
of Dùn Athad. (9)

Natural arches
at
Port nan Gallan. (10)

Port nan Gallan. (10)

Looking   south-east towards
Dùn Athad and
Port nan Gallan. (10)

Highland Cattle at
Upper Killeyan.
Beinn Mhòr in the distance. (11)

The American Monument from
Port nan Gallan. (12)

Otter feeding at
Lower Killeyan. (13)

Low tide at
Lower Killeyan. (13)

Eileanan Mòra at Lower Killeyan . (13)

Colourful stones at
Lower Killeyan. (13)

Rainbow on sea stack,
Lower Killeyan. (13)

Small beach north of
Lower Killeyan. (14)

View north towards
caves at
Astle Bay. (15)

Astle Bay looking
south-south-west. (16)

Astle Bay and caves at
Rubha Ruadh. (16)

Golden Eagle above
Rubha Ruadh in
Astle Bay. (16)

Caves at Bun an Easa. (17)

Looking
north-north-east from
Bun an Easa. (18)

Soldier's Rock. (19)

Port an Sguite,
near Kintra. (20)

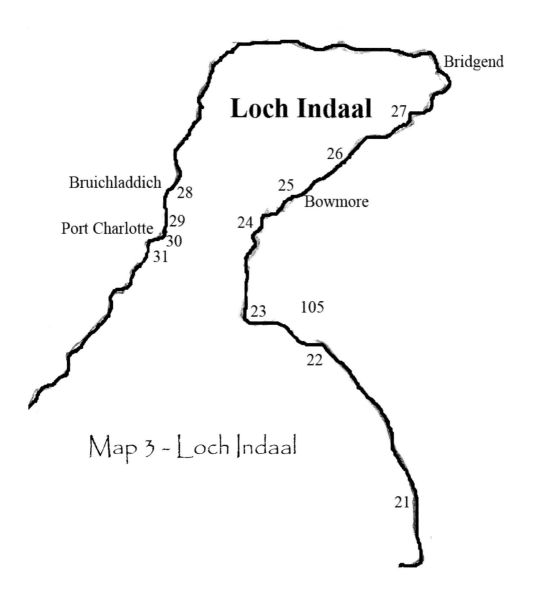

Map 3 - Loch Indaal

South end of Big Strand
looking north. (21)

North end of Big Strand,
looking south. (22)

Creag nam Fitheach (39 m) at
Laggan Point on a dull day looking
towards the
Rhinns of Islay. (23)

Gartbreck, looking across
Loch Indaal to
Port Charlotte. (24)

Bowmore pier in winter, looking up
Loch Indaal towards the
Paps of Jura. (25)

Bowmore in winter
from the east. (25)

Loch Indaal on a stormy day in September with
Bowmore on the left and
Beinn Tart a'Mhill (232 m) in the distance. (26)

Snow-covered Paps of Jura and head of Loch Indaal. (27)

Fishing boat at Bruichladdich,
looking south-east towards
Laggan Point. (28)

Port Charlotte lighthouse, looking
towards the
Paps of Jura. (29)

Port Charlotte village. (30)

Alpacas in field south of
Port Charlotte with
Laggan Point in the distance. (31)

Map 4 ~ The Rhinns

52

Wester Ellister from the
north-east. (32)

Sea fury at
Port Wemyss. (33)

Sea fury at
Port Wemyss. (33)

Sunset over Portnahaven village
and
Orsay lighthouse. (34)

Beaches and inlets
north-north-west of Portnahaven
with Claddach beach top left. (35)

Claddach Beach (Currie Sands). (36)

Inlet near
Lossit Bay. (37)

Lossit Bay. (38)

Beinn Seasaimh (139 m) looking
north-east towards the
Paps of Jura. (39)

Bun na h-Aibhne, between
Kilchiaran and
Lossit Bay. (40)

Suspended boulder
near Kilchiaran. (41)

Kilchiaran Bay. (42)

November sunset
at Kilchiaran. (42)

'Granny Rock'
between Kilchiaran
and
Machir Bay. (43)

Machir Bay from summit of
Turnaichaidh (170 m). (44)

Remains of shipwreck,
Machir Bay. (45)

Machir Bay from north with flag iris
and thrift. (46)

Inlet west of
Machir Bay. (47)

Ruin west of
Machir Bay. (48)

Inlet west of
Machir Bay. (49)

Looking north between Machir Bay and Saligo. (50)

Dry stane dyke and thrift between
Machir Bay and Saligo. (51)

Looking south between
Machir Bay and Saligo. (52)

(Previous page: top - Looking north towards Saligo and Dùn Bheolain. (53);
bottom - Flag Iris near Saligo. (53)
This page: Marsh Fritillary near Saligo. (53)

Map 5 - Gruinart

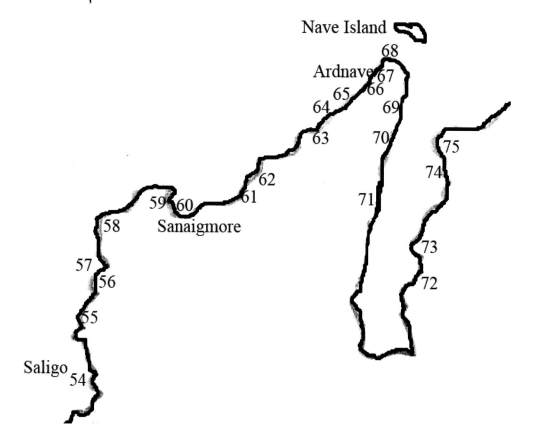

Nave Island

Ardnave

68
67
65 66
64 69
63 70
75
62 74
61 71
59 60
58 Sanaigmore
73
57 72
56
55
Saligo 54

Saligo Bay. Looking north towards Dùn Bheolain. (54)

Saligo Bay. Looking north
towards Dùn Bheolain. (54)
Opposite page: waves at Saligo. (54)

Sunset at Saligo looking north towards Dùn Bheolain. (54)

Wave fury at Saligo. (54)

Dùn Bheolain
from the south. (55)

Dùn Bheolain
from the north. (55)

Turquoise sea and pink thrift on
cliffs above Saligo. (56)

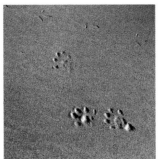

Left: Green Hairstreak. (57)
Middle: Otter tracks at Tràigh Bhàn. (57)
Right: Thrift at Tràigh Bhàn. (57)

Tràigh Bhàn -
a south-west
facing beach. (57)

Trig point on Cnoc Uamh nam Fear
(128 m) looking north-east towards
Sanaigmore and the Paps of Jura.
Colonsay is just visible on the
left of the picture. (58)

Port Ghille Greamhair -
a north-east facing beach. (59)

Sanaigmore Bay looking
north-east. (60)

Sanaigmore Bay
looking west. (60)

Barnacle Geese
at Sanaigmore. (60)

Sanderling and Ringed Plover at Sanaigmore. (60)

Sanderling at Sanaigmore. (60)

Thrift and coast north-east of
Sanaigmore. (61)

Interesting rock formations between Sanaigmore and Ardnave. (62)

Sea stacks between Sanaigmore
and Ardnave. (63)

Looking north to
Nave Island. (64)

Nave Island and Ardnave from the south-west. (65)

Previous page: Stone circle near Tràigh Nostaig, Ardnave. (66)
This Page: Tràigh Nostaig looking north-east. (67)

Ardnave - looking south-west
towards Sanaig cliffs. (68)

Mouth of Loch Gruinart with
Mala Bholsa in the distance. (69)

Loch Gruinart in February, looking north-east to the snow-covered Paps of Jura. (70)

Looking through the
window of
Kilnave Chapel. (71)

Bun-an-uilt, Loch Gruinart,
looking north-north-west. (72)

Ruin on east side of
Loch Gruinart. (73)

Killinallan sands looking
north-north-east. (74)

Harebells by
the Killinallan River. (75)

Left: Ringlet at Killinallan. (75)
Middle: Grass of Parnassus at Killinallan. (75)
Right: Common Blue on Self-heal at Killinallan.

Pyramidal Orchids at Killinallan. (75)

Looking west at
Killinallan. (75)

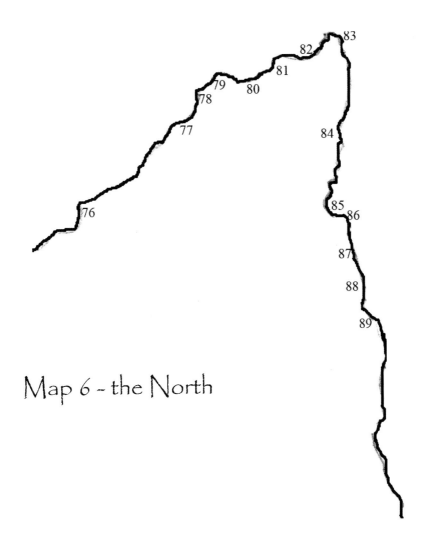

Map 6 - the North

Trig point
at Gortantoid. (76)

Caves near
Mala Bholsa. (77)

Natural arches and waterfall near
Mala Bholsa. (78)

Natural arches near
Mala Bholsa. (78)

Near Mala Bholsa. (78)

Opposite page: sunset near Mala Bholsa. (78)

View north-east from slopes of
Mala Bholsa. (79)

View east from
Port an Sruthain. (80)

Colonsay from
Islay's north coast. (81)

Bàgh an Da Dhoruis looking
south-south-west with
Mala Bholsa in the distance. (82)

Rubh a'Mhail
lighthouse from the
north-west. (83)

Waterfall
on Islay's
north-east coast. (84)

Bunnahabhain
from the north. (85)

Wreck of the 'Wyre Majestic' off
Rubh a'Mhill, Bunnahabhain. (86)

Left: Small Copper, near Caol Ila. (87)
Middle: Frog, near Caol Ila. (87)
Right: Speckled Wood, near Caol Ila. (87)

Otter south of Port Askaig. (88)

Port Bhoraraic and the
Sound of Islay with the
Paps of Jura
in the background. (89)

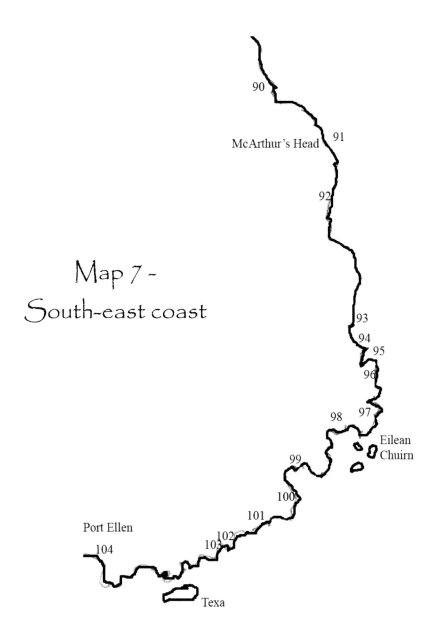

Map 7 –
South-east coast

90

McArthur's Head 91

92

93
94
95
96
97
98
Eilean
Chuirn

99

100

101

Port Ellen
102
103
104

Texa

An Cladach
on the
Sound of Islay. (90)

Sunrise over the Sound of Islay
and Jura from
An Cladach bothy. (90)

Lighthouse at McArthur's Head. (91)

Bothy at Proaig. (92)

Beach at Ardtalla. (93)

Claggain Bay and
Beinn Bheigier from the
south-east. (94)

137

Aros Bay
from the north. (95)

Aros Bay
from the south-east. (95)

Silver Birch trees
south of
Aros Bay. (96)

View west from Ardmore trigpoint, looking towards Ardmore House and Port Mòr. (97)

View north-east from
Ardmore Point (46 m), looking
towards the Sound of Islay
and Jura. (97)

Eilean Chuirn
from the west. (98)

Otter at Ardilistry Bay. (99)

Ardilistry Bay looking west
towards
Cnoc Rhaonastil (109 m). (99)

Previous page: Common Seals in Loch an t-Sàilein. (100)
This page: Ardbeg Distillery in a storm. (101)

Dunyvaig Castle. (102)

Lagavulin Distillery
from the east. (103)

Port Ellen - Loch Leòdamais. (104)

The Grand Finale –
crossing the
River Laggan
on 6th May 2008.
(105 – p 39)

(Photo: Ray Husthwaite)